HABAKKUK:
A Wrestler with God

£5-00

HABAKKUK:
A Wrestler with God

Walter J. Chantry

THE BANNER OF TRUTH TRUST

THE BANNER OF TRUTH TRUST

3 Murrayfield Road, Edinburgh EH12 6EL, UK
P.O. Box 621, Carlisle, PA 17013, USA

First published 2008

© Walter J. Chantry 2008

*

ISBN-13: 978 0 85151 995 1

*

Typeset in 11/15 pt Sabon at
the Banner of Truth Trust
Printed in the U.S.A. by
Versa Press, Inc.,
East Peoria, IL

CONTENTS

INTRODUCTION

READING THE BOOK OF HABAKKUK takes us back to the Middle East of 2,700 years ago. One's first impressions are that the prophet lived in a very different world. Technology, communication, even awareness of far-away places, differed sharply then from what they are today. Yet these are very superficial impressions.

The more one listens to the prophet and to God's words in responding to him, the more it becomes profoundly clear that the human condition was much the same then as it is now. Decent and religious Jews were anguished at the forms of societal change in their own nation. Recent transformations in the lifestyles of their beloved country were displaying deeply evil tendencies of departing from God and of inflicting harm upon their fellow men.

As though these worrisome developments were not enough to bear, an even heavier weight was pressing down on Habakkuk and his friends. Israel was sharing life on our globe with tyrannical nations amassing armies of overwhelming size and power which were bent on brutal aggression against the Jewish people and those of other nations. Troubles in national affairs and fear of international developments! Was life so very different from our own times?

Yet how many today, with escalating concerns similar to Habakkuk's, respond as he did? Many rouse themselves to political activity, raising the volume of their voices to their fellow men in the hope of contributing to solutions. How many have recognized that moral and religious decay is so far advanced in Western Europe and the Americas that our only hope to arrest the slide is in the Lord who made Heaven and Earth? Our voices must be raised to our God, or complete collapse may not be far off.

Weary and weakened by bloody and costly wars brought upon our nations by tyrants, we have neither national resolve nor sufficient treasure to expend against enemy nations. Yet these foreign powers spend their wealth to arm with ever more horrific weapons, as they make threats against our religion and our way of life.

A few will claim that we have moral and material resources to continue a succession of brutal conflicts. Others would rather deny the existence of the threats or surrender to oppression. But unless the Lord arises to our aid how will we survive the terrors which stalk us?

If we as Western nations stand in such acute need of divine assistance on every hand, where are those who can grapple with God to bring *him* to our aid? There still are many who raise varied petitions to God's throne in prayer. But how few can take hold of God and not let him go until he blesses us! How many will continue with determination to call on the Lord and then watch for his answers until salvation is sure?

When in the past the circumstances of God's people suggested that inescapable doom was approaching, their Shepherd promised to work mighty wonders of salvation for them. However, as he did so the Sovereign over all the earth said, 'I will yet for this be inquired of by the house of Israel, to do it for them' (*Ezek.* 36:37, KJV). The Almighty expected human prayer to be a secondary agent for his most astounding deliverances. Always the Creator is himself the First Cause.

In times of emergency we wonder if we *can* pray. The reason for this was noted by the Apostle Paul: 'For we do not know what to pray for as we ought' (*Rom.* 8:26b). We know what we want! But we are too unfamiliar with entering the courts of the King of Glory, looking him in the eye, and bringing to him our great requests. An urgent need of our time and place in history is for 'the Spirit to help us in our weakness' (*Rom.* 8:26a). We require 'the Spirit interceding for us according to the will of God' (*Rom.* 8:27).

In this great book of divine revelation we draw back the curtain over the prayer chamber of a man of God. We listen to him pray. We listen as God responds in one of his remarkable revelations. However, you may be stunned by the actual answers to his prayers!

There is one other tie between Habakkuk's age and our own. The Lord used the Book of Habakkuk as the strongbox into which he placed one of the most precious gems of all time (*Hab.* 2:4). It is a sentence which summarizes the gospel. It is, in fact, a gemstone of four facets which brilliantly displays the following four qualities: *faith, humility, righteousness* and *eternal life.*

The Apostle Paul was accustomed to using this verse as the theme of his gospel instruction and as the corrective to false teaching (*Rom.* 1:17, *Gal.* 3:11, *Heb.* 10:38).

Although we have no record of Jesus' actually quoting the passage from Habakkuk, if the verse is used as a filter through which the Gospels are read its emphasis will be found throughout the Saviour's ministry. In Matthew 8:5–13 we have an account of a man who sought Jesus' assistance. His requests of our Lord were made with the deepest humility. Of this humble man Jesus remarked, 'With no one in Israel have I found such faith.' There followed a comment about Gentiles entering the kingdom of God.

When you find this verse, pause and ponder over it. Search there whether you have been made righteous, whether you have eternal life.

WALTER J. CHANTRY
April 2008

1

A Prophet's Burden (1:1–4)

THIS PROPHETIC BOOK, like most others in the Old Testament, bears the title of the prophet's name. Habakkuk is a form of the Hebrew word 'embrace'. The idea is of a wrestler in an embrace with the opponent with whom he is contending. This book is about a man who lived out his name by wrestling with God in prayer. Our text is unique among prophetic books. It is a diary of three prayers by Habakkuk and two answers by the Most High God, one for each of the first two prayers.

THE MAN OF GOD

We find similarities between ourselves and Habakkuk as we read his prayer journal. At times through Scripture we have 'seen' things which deeply trouble our spirits. The weight of these burdens compels us to wrestle with God in prayer. Yet we are *not* like Habakkuk! He had a calling from God to be 'the prophet' (1:1). God Almighty set him aside to be *God's* spokesman, to declare the very words of *God*. He was God's mouthpiece to deliver a divine message to the world. He was a 'holy man' 'carried along by the Holy Spirit' (2 *Pet.* 1:21). Habakkuk's words were 'breathed out' by God himself through his prophet (2 *Tim.* 3:16). No part of this book is a matter of Habakkuk's 'private interpretation' (2 *Pet.* 1:20). Though we also wrestle with God in prayer, these things are never true of us.

Even when Habakkuk 'saw' (1:1), it was not like our seeing. The Holy Spirit does enlighten the eyes of our understanding through Scripture. Prophets, however, were (in the earliest days) called 'Seers' (*1 Sam.* 9:9, *2 Sam.* 24:11).

In Numbers 12:6 the Lord said to Aaron and Miriam, 'If there is a prophet among you, I, the LORD, make Myself known to him in a vision, I speak in a dream. Not so My servant Moses . . . I speak with him face to face.' God made prophets to see truth directly in visions and dreams.

Those things which they saw, they conveyed to us in words of Scripture. The exceptions were Moses and the Prophet like Moses, Jesus Christ (*Deut.* 18:18). These two spoke with God face-to-face and delivered more clear and complete messages in Holy Scripture.

Usually the 'burden' (1:1) of a prophet was a heavy spiritual weight. It was heavy because of the content of his tidings, most often a clear vision of coming judgments. This book of Habakkuk declares judgments to come. It was also a heaviness of responsibility to declare to men on earth what the God of Heaven had shown him. On one occasion the Prophet Jeremiah resolved not to declare the message God had given him. Jeremiah remarked of that resolve, 'But His word was in my heart like a burning fire shut up in my bones; I was weary of holding it back, and I could not' (*Jer.* 20:9). Habakkuk was delivering *heavy* things.

A COMPLAINT ABOUT GOD'S ANSWERING OF PRAYER

The first recorded prayer of Habakkuk is in 1:2–4. The journal does not begin at the beginning. The prophet had been praying about the matter on his heart for some time before his diary of prayer began. There is a bluntness to the Hebrew protest which does not quite come through in English: 'How long, Jehovah, have I cried, and You do not listen? I cry to You . . . and You do not help' (1:2)!

Habakkuk was deeply disturbed with the national sins of Judah. He frequently and earnestly cried to God for relief, but no deliverance came. He had taken the matter before the throne of God, but no improvement appeared. It seemed as if God did not hear prayer or that he refused to answer it. Perhaps you remember the way in which Elijah mocked the prophets of Baal when their prayers brought no fire from heaven. 'He is busy, or he is on a journey, or perhaps he is sleeping and must be awakened' (1 *Kings* 18:27).

What began as an appeal for God's salvation for his nation ended as a personal protest about God's inaction. Habakkuk was right to take the national evils before the throne of God. Too many trust in princes and seek aid from men. They expect political appeals and protests to bring reformation. Habakkuk took his protest into the courts of the Sovereign over all the earth. But there seemed to be no response. He was compelled to pray about the process of prayer. Are there no times when *you* are frustrated in your prayers' return of silence? How long must we face heavens of brass?

A COMPLAINT ABOUT GOD'S RULE OF THIS WORLD

Perhaps there were evil secondary causes of the moral decay and social misery of Habakkuk's time. However, our theology directs our attention to the ultimate cause – divine providence. 'Why do You make me see iniquity? Why do You tolerate injustice' (1:3)? After all is said, God has placed us in a corrupt and provoking nation at a time when he is permitting morals to plunge to ever-lower depths and permitting the church to become ever weaker. He has appointed that we live through such times filled with sorrow and distress. It is a time when God has given up formerly Christian nations to spiritual darkness and uncleanness. Our prayers have not reversed these trends. Why? That is also what Habakkuk is asking God. 'Why?'

Habakkuk was probably living in the last twenty years of the Seventh Century BC. These were years subsequent to the most wicked and defiling reign of any king of Judah, that of Manasseh. Jeremiah was one of the prophet's contemporaries. Vice of every kind was pandemic. Unbelief was rampant.

Is it not a modern complaint of God's people today that our western culture is descending to ever-lower moral and religious disgrace? This is something we grumble about to one another. Are you expressing your heartache over these matters to God? Only he has the power to reverse such trends. So many prayer meetings are filled with petitions about sickness and asking for God's blessing on our future plans. Should we not cry to God against the evil of the times and persist in it? Do ministers in their pulpit prayers rehearse the moral and religious atrocities of our age and ask God to arise and correct these alarming trends?

NAMING THE PRECISE DEPRAVITIES OF HABAKKUK'S NATION

As we notice the prayer of the prophet we identify with his anguish, knowing similar evils in our times. 'Violence' (1:2) is his first-mentioned feature of life in his nation. It is re-emphasized in verse 3: 'Plundering and violence are before me.' He seems to pray with a sense of horror. Shall we list violent abortions, violent euthanasia, battering of wives and children, shootings in schools by fellow-students and sexual predators, bombings, riots, and road rage?

These crimes are increasing in formerly Christian nations of the West. There is violence from drug trafficking, violence in love triangles. How long before God helps us?

Then the prophet lists injustice to the innocent and helpless (1:4):

> The law is powerless,
> And justice never goes forth.
> For the wicked surround the righteous;
> Therefore perverse judgment proceeds.

In his nation, as in ours, the legal system worked in behalf of the wicked rather than the righteous. With us, governmental laws and the judges who interpret them defend the rights of pornographers and rebuke any who would deny them freedom to promote their vices. The system protects sexual perverts at great cost to public health. Courts threaten parents who correct and discipline their children. State education inculcates unbelief and scepticism and silences biblical opinions. Why is God not listening to our appeals?

Surely you can share Habakkuk's tensions as he prayed. You can sense the inner temptation to unbelief which would lead us to cease praying. You may feel equally frustrated by a lifetime of praying for the advancement of truth and righteousness in our generation without God's arising to help. Are you still grappling with God over these very same elements of our national life? These are huge difficulties which only a great God can resolve. We must pray on. Our only help is in the name of the Lord who made the heavens and the earth. Our hope of blessing *must be fixed upon him*.

Remember that this is only the opening entry in Habakkuk's prayer log. The prayer struggle between the prophet and his God continues. It will end with prayers of confidence and triumph.

> The LORD God is my strength;
> He will make my feet like deer's feet,
> And He will make me walk on my high hills
> *Habakkuk* 3:19

The process leading to such a calm and hopeful state was not pleasant to him, and it may not be for us. This prophecy is for our time as well as for an ancient era. Were Habakkuk to have had the benefit of specific revelation given by God 650 years after his time, he might have realized that God was not inactive toward rebellious Judah as it seemed to the prophet. It was Paul, in Romans 1:18–32, who taught us that, when nations are far advanced in rejecting God's revelation and in moral corruption, God does not always hasten either to reform them or to destroy them.

Often, when it still seems to us that God has not acted toward evil nations, the first wave of divine wrath against the evil has already begun. The Holy One 'gives up' wicked societies 'to uncleanness' (*Rom.* 1:24), 'to vile passions' (*Rom.* 1:26). Removing all providential restraints from the wicked tendencies of fallen sinners, the Lord allows human depravity to run to its most degraded expressions until a nation is 'filled with all unrighteousness' (*Rom.* 1:29).

That God does sometimes judge in this fashion is hinted at in Genesis 15:16. Here was an awesome scene in which God reiterated his promise to give Abram the land of Canaan. The Lord explained that Abram's descendants must be servants in another land for four hundred years. This was because 'the sin of the Amorites had not yet reached its full measure' (NIV). Only when iniquity had done its full work would final judgment fall on the Amorites. God permitting such a descent by degrees into sin was a ripening for more active expressions of wrath.

However, in the inscrutable purposes of God, sinners are sometimes permitted to express very high degrees of wickedness before God arises to save them. A very evil Manasseh was allowed to demonstrate to everyone the shameful baseness of his heart before God transformed him into a godly man (2 *Chron.* 33:1–20). Saul of Tarsus ran to the full extent of his defiled nature – publicly blaspheming the Son of God and violently doing his utmost to destroy the Church of Christ – before the Saviour made him a new man and an apostle to the Gentiles! In such cases chief sinners grow worse and worse to demonstrate to all people that God's sovereign mercy and grace are far mightier than all men's sins.

God had in fact been responding to Habakkuk's prayer all the while. Of course the prophet's prayer was that the Lord would save (1:1), not that he would give Judah up to destruction. In the case of this nation, the even worse sinfulness would not issue in final judgment but in chastisement leading to mercy. Much later, as Jew and Gentile alike reached a fullness of unrighteousness in the violent assault on Messiah, God sent the mighty gospel into all benighted nations. However, the prophet could not foresee the purposes of God for Judah in his generation or in the days of Christ until the Lord showed him.

We must never view God as tolerating or being willing to countenance sin (1:3) as Habakkuk's prayer suggested. As unbelief and immorality intensify within our nations, the Almighty's wrath is already being revealed from heaven against all ungodliness and unrighteousness of men who suppress the truth because of their love of their sins (*Rom.* 1:18).

Until God's providence works further in the deepening spiritual and moral darkness, we cannot tell whether our nations will be utterly destroyed as they deserve to be or whether God's grace will yet arise to renew them in that true religion and righteousness which exalt nations and magnify his grace.

If the last is to be the case, God will revive them through the means of his saints' prayers, which arise in the believing wrestler's embrace of God during these hours of midnight blackness.

2

Divine Instruments of Justice (1:5–11)

HABAKKUK HAD LONG PRAYED against the sins
of God's special nation – Judah. Like most
of us, he was a patriot. He loved his nation,
and he loved the saints who lived within his home-
land. Living through an extended season of moral
decay and spiritual corruption had made the prophet
hunger for revival.

It was not merely to bring relief for himself from
the discomforts of living on sin's playground that he
prayed. There was also the question of what kind of
land would be left to his children and grandchildren.
'Righteousness exalts a nation, but sin is a reproach
to any people' (*Prov.* 14:34). Destruction awaits the
godless. 'The wicked shall be turned into hell, and
all the nations that forget God' (*Psa.* 9:17).

If only the Lord would make the ministries of
priests and prophets powerful and effective to turn

the tide to righteousness and to bring God's blessing! This was the longing of Habakkuk's heart.

When we genuinely enter into long-sustained prayer about our national declension from morals and religion, we are wrestling with the history of God's providence. How, we wonder, can the Holy One tolerate the multiplying of wickedness; how can he refuse to heed the prayers of the godly?

In Habakkuk 1:5–11, the Almighty broke the long silence toward the praying prophet. In this short text God gave a specific answer. It was a direct, verbal revelation about the near future (we do *not* receive such revelations now, though perhaps by the Holy Spirit's aid we receive insight as to how biblical texts apply to our present circumstances).

A WARNING LABEL

It was necessary for the Most High to precede his answer with cautionary preparations. The observer of coming history must be conditioned to interpret rightly the plainest truths.

The essence of all that God told Habakkuk was, 'I share your concern about godliness and morality in Judah' (and *yours* if you are praying – in Europe, in the Americas, or elsewhere, in the twenty-first century). 'I am preparing a definite response to this infidelity toward me and to its expression in widespread lawbreaking.'

Divine Instruments of Justice (1:5–11)

1. *You will have to look at the nations for the chosen solution:* 'Look among the nations, and watch . . . For I will work a work in your days' (*Hab.* 1:5). You are so focused on your local interest. Look to international affairs. Our God is Lord of all nations. His purposes are global! Did not Jehovah tell Abraham, 'In your seed all the nations of the earth shall be blessed' (*Gen.* 22:18)?

God had not forgotten Judah. Yet Judah was not God's only interest, nor was she his only love. No! God's answers are *not* always seen in the sending of revival. Sometimes they appear by way of multi-national events.

2. *As you look at international news, do not forget what the news reporters seldom say.* 'I am working' (verse 5) what you observe. 'I am raising up' a new power among the nations (verse 6). In answer to your prayers and to correct the deplorable religious and moral decline in your land, I am empowering a heathen nation! What occurs across the face of the whole earth has been designed by God's eternal, intelligent plan. All kings' hearts are in God's hand, to be turned into the course of God's choice. When great armies assemble and begin to march, they are under the dominion and direction of our God. Watch these international events! Know that all of them are directed from God's throne. We have the book of

nature in which we read of God's creative power. We have the book of Scripture in which we read of God's redemptive power. We also have the book of current events in which we read the outworking of God's providential purposes.

3. *God is at work 'in your days'* (verse 5) to do something about Judah's rebellion (and in our days to do something about rebellion in the West). The text speaks of events that will occur during Habakkuk's lifetime. He would see some of the Lord's works with his own eyes. So shall we.

4. *Habakkuk would have found the prediction incredible.* 'Be utterly astounded!' (verse 5). 'For I will work a work in your days which you would not believe though it were told you.' Even God's people are inclined not to believe what they never wish to see. God would not solve Judah's moral crisis by Habakkuk's preferred method of revival! He would solve it in unexpected and undesirable ways.

When we pray about the slippery slope of modern western irreverence toward God and immorality toward fellow-citizens, we advise God to handle our case with gentle kindness. We hope for a 'soft landing', for a 'happy ending'. This is not always preferable to our God. After his people's long years of massive defection from faith, from decency and

14

from justice our Maker and Judge may prefer an appropriate solution which stuns us.

CHASTISEMENT FROM GOD IS DESCRIBED

For Judah, God was raising up the nation of Babylon (verse 6). A new world-dominating power was being formed to execute God's will among the nations. Its armies would be the instrument God would use to bring final destruction to nations whose measure of sin had become full. Some enemies of Babylon would cease to exist as nations. In Judah's case violent defeat at the hands of Babylon would be a severe chastisement. Plundering of the nation and deportation of its people would be a means to Judah's spiritual improvement. Just as a father cannot always correct gently, so also the Lord must use the infliction of pain to call his people back to a fear of his name and to a more righteous course of conduct.

Had Habakkuk searched diligently in Scripture he might have guessed what God would do to his nation. Seven hundred years earlier Moses had written in Deuteronomy 28, 'If you do not obey the voice of the LORD your God . . . the LORD will bring a nation against you from afar . . . as swift as the eagle flies, a nation whose language you will not understand, a nation of fierce countenance . . .

Then the LORD will scatter you among all peoples, from one end of the earth to the other.'

Then, only one hundred years before Habakkuk lived, God had spoken to Hezekiah, king of Judah, through Isaiah the prophet: 'Behold the days are coming when all that is in your house, and what your fathers have accumulated until this day, shall be carried to Babylon; nothing shall be left, says the LORD' (*Isa.* 39:6).

A BRIEF HISTORY OF BABYLON

For centuries Babylon had been a small state, little involved in international affairs. Although it was the location of the first historic attempt to form a one-world government not long after the Flood (the tower of Babel, *Gen.* 11:1–9), Babylon began building an army only in the year 626 BC. In 609 BC Babylonian conquests began to alarm Assyria (whose capital was Nineveh) and Egypt, the two great centres of world power. These two nations united to attack certain Babylonian outposts. The Babylonian king, Nabopolassar, however, held his ground at the Euphrates River. In a sense the battle was a stand-off, although in truth it would prove to be a last gasp of power for both Assyria and Egypt.

In that very year of 609 BC, Josiah, king of Judah, had died, and his son Jehoahaz had been crowned in Jerusalem. However, on his way back to Egypt from the battle with Babylon, Pharaoh Necho deposed Jehoahaz and installed Jehoiakim as Egypt's servant-king in Judah. With this event Judah's genuine independence as a nation ceased until AD 1948.

In 605 BC Babylon was led into battle at Carchemish by Crown Prince Nebuchadnezzar. Again the foes were Assyria and Egypt whose combined forces were utterly smashed by Babylon. The balance of power among the nations had dramatically shifted, never to return to Assyria or to Egypt. Following this great triumph, Nebuchadnezzar made his first incursion into Israel, also in 605 BC. It was in this military conquest that Daniel, Shadrach, Meshach and Abednego (then young teenagers) were marched off to Babylon along with much of the royalty of Judah. Two later invasions by Babylon, in 596 BC and 586 BC, would further depopulate the nation of Judah and leave the city of Jerusalem in ruins with its temple demolished.

Babylon gave new meaning to the word 'empire'. A series of heathen world powers – Babylon, Persia, Greece, and Rome – would control Palestine, along with most of the civilized world, for nine hundred years until the reign of Jesus Christ ended these horrors. Babylon was the rod of the Almighty to punish disobedient and depraved nations. Babylon was the axe in the hand of the Most High to cut down the tree of Judah at the height of its pride and idolatry. Although such world empires have not reappeared since the fall of Rome, many nations have aspired to like achievements, and in doing so have, on a smaller scale, served the same purpose of God to judge and to chasten evil societies.

CHARACTERISTICS OF WARRING NATIONS

In Habakkuk 1:6–11 the Lord described for the prophet what Judah might expect at the hands of their fellow-men. If nations will imagine that life is to be preferred without 'interference' from the God of Heaven, consider what such countries experience at the hands of their fellow-men when the Almighty's restraining hand is removed from their enemies. Babylon would be *ruthless*, ill-tempered, acting out of bitterness, and lacking in compassion (verse 6). They would be *impetuous*. Their cruelty would be irrational, like that of a bear robbed of her cubs (verse 6). This army would sweep in all directions, like none had done before her. There would be no serious challenge at all to her power.

So too would the invaders be greedy for plunder (verse 6). They would be eager to seize that to which they had no claim. 'Terrible and dreadful' would they be (verse 7). All who faced them would recoil in fear. They would be lawless, following no international conventions of war. All rules of engagement would originate with themselves alone (verse 7). Arrogance and pride would be their guides.

The assaults of these armies would be swifter than leopards rushing suddenly upon their prey (verse 8). Their soldiers would be like evening wolves for fierceness -- tearing apart their victims in the darkness (verse 8). These armies were like eagles swiftly flying to devour (verse 8).

They would be bent upon violence (verse 9), sweeping like the wind, scooping up prisoners as grains of sand. Displacement of the population was their settled method of dominance. Babylonian warriors crushed kings and laughed at fortifications (verse 10). From these rapid and wild assaults they rushed on to their next foes. Not only would they conquer Judah, but they would defeat *all* the nations round them. They worshipped their own prowess (verse 11). In short, they had made a god of human might.

This was God's work *then*, and he is the same *yesterday, today, and forever*. As Judge of all the earth he is impartial. He has always been patient with sinners, as he calls men to repentance. But he also is a God of great wrath against the sins of the nations. Nebuchadnezzar began his conquests against Judah at God's direction. Peter said, 'The time has come for judgment to begin at the house of God; and if it begins with us first, what will be the end of those who do not obey the gospel?' (*1 Pet.* 4:17).

Habakkuk was being told that God *would* bring savage war upon the prophet's beloved nation, a people who had rejected the God of their fathers. As we look at current events and the near future of our nations we do not have the advantage of revelation to delineate what God is about to do. But we do know from this prophecy that, at times, God brings brutal armies against fallen churches, societies and nations to correct their foolishness.

Nations of the West have largely renounced the faith of their fathers of former days. Secular government has been chosen over the fear of God in national affairs. The most depraved and heathen practices fill our culture and our educational systems. Churches imitate the world rather than following God's Word in worship. All of this is taking place amidst a refusal to admit that we are vulnerable to the wrath of man and of God.

Nations to our east are gathering strength. These nations have false gods; they are brutal, ambitious, and increasing in military power. Such nations have served as rods of the Almighty to be used on the backs of his wayward people.

Will not even the seriousness of the threats lead God's people to repentance? Must there not be such humiliation of spirit in us to bring revival which may return the western nations to their senses? Without such humility and sorrow for sins a yet more bitter reminder of God's seriousness in his programme for the earth will surely fall upon us.

3

Great Prayers in Devastating Times (1:12–2:1)

W E IN THE MODERN WESTERN NATIONS stand in a position similar to that of Habakkuk in ancient times. As we examine our own culture we observe that the majority of 'Christian churches' are distant from believing scriptural doctrine and keeping God's commandments. Governmental and educational systems are hostile to God's truth. Therefore immorality is rampant and genuine Christians are despised. Every institution of our society is enfeebled through drifting without a moral compass.

At the same time, as we look in the direction of the eastward nations we observe self-conscious enemies to the foundations of western civilization rising. God is raising up fierce destructive powers who worship false gods. They are brutal and aggressive; they are instilling in their people hatred toward both the

God of our fathers and the corrupted descendants of these fathers, who can neither comprehend their danger nor rouse themselves to repentance or even to self-defence.

Habakkuk asked in his first prayer 'how long' (1:2) God would do nothing about the evils in Israel. The King of glory broke his silence to say that soon (verse 6) Habakkuk's land would be chastised with the rod of Babylonian cruelty. God's answer and action were to be seen in international affairs. Not a native godly prophet, effective in preaching, but a pitiless, savage army from afar would correct God's unfaithful people. We have no such revelation for today; but we do have the precedent of God's former ways to make us fear.

Under the shock of a revelation so calamitous for Judah, Habakkuk prayed again. It is our second recorded prayer of his book (*Hab.* 1:12–2:1). So too should we pray under the twin clouds of deepening departure from God and his ways in our homelands and of threatenings of war from foreign powers. Judah's prophet may give form to appropriate modern prayers in circumstances similar to his own.

HABAKKUK'S CONCEPTION OF PRAYER

Habakkuk was persuaded that what was happening in his beloved fatherland was under the dominion of God's throne. Furthermore what was revealed of the future history of the nations fell under God's direct authority. The clash of powerful armies on earth represented the unfolding of God's holy will. Jehovah is a most pure spiritual Being whose purposes come to pass upon the earth.

Therefore there is no more vital activity that Habakkuk can undertake than conversation with the One who directs current events. Similarly, although we may be perplexed at God's direction of history and may be unable to comprehend why he is doing as he does, there must never be a question that in prayer we speak with the Creator of heaven and earth. Our discussion engages the Person presiding over future events. Even when we and Habakkuk do not receive exactly what we want from God, the Most High over our times and nations is listening to us and answering.

Furthermore the Most High God employs human prayer in executing his purposes. God invites and commands human words of discussion with him to serve as a means to accomplishing his divine decrees. Prayer links the human mind and the divine mind in accomplishing God's mighty acts. Of course we contribute no wisdom or power to God's governance. Yet, prayer makes human will and divine will flow together in directing planet Earth. It is God who devised prayer before his throne to be involved in the carrying through of his workings. His is all the power and glory, but he invites us by prayer to participate in the decisions of his heavenly throne.

Failure to hold such a view of prayer makes men dull and silent as they come to pray. Such ignorance empties church prayer meetings. It robs men of hope that things will change in the future. Without prayer men move about as uninvolved robots in their rounds of life. Earthbound men are out of touch with the Father of spirits. Their atrophied souls lie unused.

We were made in the image of God to commune with him, speaking with him whose arm directs all events. How many believers chatter to other men about national moral crises and international threats poised to crush God's people! Nonetheless, too many have fled from God's throne room where their voices would do much good.

PRAYER: REHEARSING TRUTHS OF WHICH WE ARE CERTAIN

In our most desperate hours there are truths of which we are fully assured. These should be affirmed to the Lord.

> Are You not from everlasting,
> O LORD my God, my Holy One?
> . . . O LORD . . . O Rock . . .
> *Habakkuk* 1:12

With warm affection Habakkuk expressed direct attachment to the Most High: You are *my* God and *my* Holy One. I cleave to you in these distressing hours. Our bond is not broken. When all else gives way you, O Lord, are the Rock upon which I have firm footing.

God's sovereignty reaches back to eternity. His purposes, even to appoint wild, heathen Babylonians to attack and to dismantle Judah, were no hasty decision of the moment. Yet, in the same recesses of eternity God's purposes of grace were linked with the seed of Abraham and the seed of David. Thus the affirmation, 'We shall not die.'

Whatever disasters befell Israel at the hands of marauders, the people of God could not be exterminated. Just so in modern times the very gates of Hell cannot prevail against Christ's church. These things are certainties. Though Judah then and the church now may be rebuked and corrected by fearful enemies at God's appointment, they will never be annihilated. His Word has told us of his everlasting designs for them.

Sometimes in prayer we must restate our deepest convictions. It is not merely a remedial exercise for ourselves. If we intend to wrestle with God, making complaints about his providences, we must lay a proper foundation of submission and trust for our prayers.

PRAYER: GRAPPLING WITH GOD AGAINST HIS CHOSEN CORRECTION

In verse 12, Habakkuk called the Lord 'my Holy One'. The prophet was utterly confident that his God was holy. From this bedrock certainty he would launch questions about God's revealed purposes.

> You are of purer eyes than to behold evil,
> And cannot look on wickedness.
> Why do You look on those who deal treacherously,
> And hold Your tongue when the wicked devours
> A person more righteous than he?
>
> *Habakkuk 1:13*

In context the words translated 'behold' and 'look on' would better be translated 'countenance'. Of course we know that God 'sees' every wicked act of both man and demon. Yet the Almighty cannot look on them with approval or favour. How can God see and hold his tongue when the evil devour those more righteous than they? At this point the grappler (Habakkuk) has taken hold of God's holiness to argue against the Lord's plan to use the Babylonian army to ravage Judah. What a bold statement made to the very face of the Almighty!

It seemed to Habakkuk that God's tolerance of Babylon was inconsistent with his holiness. The Lord was allowing the more wicked to swallow up the less so. Where was God's holiness in this? Especially in

God's intention to be silent ('hold Your tongue')? One who witnesses a sin and remains silent partakes of the guilt of the sin (*Lev.* 5:1). How could God keep quiet as Nebuchadnezzar swallowed Jerusalem and marched righteous Daniel, Shadrach, Meshach, Abednego, and Ezekiel off into exile? Silent while holy Jeremiah poured out lamentations?

The prophet in prayer then poetically elaborated the holocaust which Judah would soon endure. Because of our short-sightedness toward the sweep of history we refer to the atrocities of Hitler's Third Reich against the Jews as *the* holocaust. It was only one of many. There was a holocaust for the Jews under Assyria, one under Babylon, one under Rome, and another perpetrated during the Second World War. It remains true in our day that shrill anti-Semitism threatens the Jews of Israel and elsewhere.

Habakkuk gave us a vivid and accurate description of Babylonian conquest. Men made in the image of God would be caught like fish, with hooks and dragnets. Babylonian art pictured these aftermaths of victory in the same terms. Those captured and marched off into captivity were strung together with literal hooks thrust through each person's lower lip. Such cruelty was proudly celebrated by the captors. No pity was shown to the defeated. False gods were worshipped as giving Babylon remarkable power over a multitude of nations as they relentlessly 'fished' for more victims. The prophet prays against the worst of human depravity that was crushing the civilized world.

A STEP BACK

Habakkuk was fully aware that his boldness in prayer bordered on brazenness before God. He had not quite charged God with sin. He did, however, argue that the means the Lord chose to chasten Judah were apparently inconsistent with his holiness. Still, the man of prayer fully expected the dialogue to continue. God would answer the prayer. The prophet took a defensive stance expecting God to rebuke him for such brashness:

> I will stand my watch
> And set myself on the rampart,
> And watch to see what He will say to me,
> And what I will answer when I am corrected.
> *Habakkuk* 2:1

God answers prayer. Do you watch and wait for divine replies? When you are bold and pleading with God, do you think that your ignorant and wilful assertions before the throne of heaven may draw the Father's displeasure? Do you brace yourself for an unfavourable answer? There are undulations of spirit in which we boldly plead our cause (especially as massive human disasters are near), and then we stand in fear that even our prayers have not pleased the Lord.

At this point the dialogue is not completed. God has more to say. So does Habakkuk.

4

A Revelation for All Time (2:2–4)

HABAKKUK WAS IN A VIGILANT POSTURE (*Hab*. 2: 2–4). He was fully expecting a response from the Most High to his prayer. The prophet's words had bordered on impudence in conversation with the Almighty.

It had been suggested that the Holy One surely could not stand by in silence as heathen atrocities were unleashed against a guilty (but less wicked) Israel. The prophet fully anticipated being corrected by God himself. The man of God who prayed for his nation's salvation was not disappointed. Jehovah 'answered' him (*Hab*. 2:2) quite soon. Yet, to his surprise, there was no note of rebuke from the Lord. Out of the prophet's wrestling 'embrace'[1] with God was to come a revelation central to the message of Scripture.

---

[1] The meaning of the name 'Habakkuk' is 'embrace'.

THE NATURE OF THE BIBLE

God spoke with Moses 'face to face, even plainly' (*Num.* 12:6). In the same way the Father spoke to his Son who dwelt in his bosom (*1 Cor.* 13:12, *John* 1:18). However, to many the Lord made himself known 'in a vision' or 'in a dream' (*Num.* 12:6). The Lord's answer to Habakkuk came in the form of 'vision'. God's first words to him were a command to 'write the vision' (*Hab.* 2:2) which was about to begin. The God of the whole earth designed a written revelation of himself and of his purposes which would provide mankind with his own mind disclosed in written human words. He was consciously authoring Scripture. Therefore all its sayings are God-breathed.

The product of this book of Habakkuk is not an offering of man's own original thought, nor did it originate from his own will (*2 Pet.* 1:20–21). It was from the Lord's initiative that Habakkuk wrote. The message was given to him in a vision by the will of God. Consequently, as with all Scripture, this book contains qualities that mere human writings cannot reflect.

God is concerned here, as everywhere else in the Bible, about the clarity of his revelation. 'Make it plain' (*Hab.* 2:3). Many ancient religions were 'mystery sects'. These claimed to have truth, but their writings were encrypted. Only the initiated had the secret code by which to understand the truth. God spoke in such a way as to be understood plainly. He was not hiding secrets. Jesus said, 'What you hear in the ear, preach on the housetops' (*Matt.* 10:27). The church is the 'pillar . . . of the truth' (*1 Tim.* 3:15), holding its teachings aloft for all to see.

A modern version of mystery religions is found in the suggestion that no ordinary person can read the Bible and understand it. We must have scholars who unlock the truth through their studies of archaeology, ancient history, or poetic forms that hide the real meaning. This takes the Bible away from the common man and makes him fully dependent on the priesthood of the academic community. Through this method a different interpretation is today placed on the very doctrine Habakkuk was to write plainly,[2] so that messengers who run may read it to the multitudes (*Hab.* 2:2).

Also God asserts the complete reliability of his Scripture. 'It will not lie' (*Hab.* 2:3). There is nothing deceptive in God's words. As Jesus taught, 'The Scripture cannot be broken' (*John* 10:35). In the Bible is no mixture of error with truth. 'It will surely come' (*Hab.* 2:3). It will come to pass as it was spoken. The glory of man (his scholarship and

[2] We speak of the 'new perspectives' on the doctrine of justification in which recent scholars declare that we can only understand if we have thoroughly studied 'Second-Temple' rabbinical views.

theories) will wither and fall away, 'but the word of the Lord endures forever' (*1 Pet.* 1:24–25).

THE PROFOUND REVELATION TO HABAKKUK

> Behold the proud,
> His soul is not upright in him;
> But the just, through his faith, will live.
>
> *Habakkuk* 2:4

There are only two kinds of men who have ever lived on the earth: *men of pride* and *men of faith*. This contrast is the key to history which unlocks the meaning of every generation living on the earth. Into this statement are swept all of the Old Testament and New Testament eras.

1. The proud person is not upright and thus is destined to die.
2. The just shall live through his faith.

There are three contrasts either stated or implied between the two categories of men:

1. The proud is contrasted with the believing (person of faith).
2. The 'not upright' (or unjust) is contrasted with the just.
3. One is destined to die, the other to live.

It is this contrast between pride and faith on which our Lord Jesus expanded in his teaching of justification. As our Saviour observed people 'who trusted in themselves that they were righteous and despised others' (*Luke* 18:9), he taught the parable of 'two men who went up to the temple to pray'. The Pharisee did not really pray to God, but 'with himself'. True prayer to God arises out of a sense of personal inadequacy which relies upon God for help. Instead the Pharisee boasted to God of his superiority to other men and of his religious achievements (*Luke* 18:11–12).

In evident contrast, the tax collector hesitated to draw near to God, because his conscience was smitten with guilt and shame. He confessed that he was 'the sinner', pleading with God to be propitiated (or appeased) toward him through the appointed sacrifice (*Luke* 18:13).

Whereas the Pharisee was self-confident and self-assertive before God, the tax collector had 'no confidence in the flesh' (*Phil.* 3:3). He relied entirely on God's pardoning grace through a sacrifice which satisfied divine justice with respect to his sins. Because the tax collector trusted only in God for pardon, he 'went down to his house justified' (*Luke* 18:14). His justification was immediate in the sight of God upon his expression of faith.

Our Lord added to his teaching the principle which explains human experience: 'For everyone who exalts himself will be humbled, and he who humbles himself will be exalted' (*Luke* 18:14). Pride is the precise opposite of faith, as Habakkuk has written plainly.

Furthermore, the apostle Paul quoted Habakkuk 2:4 as the theme of his great Epistle to the Romans (*Rom.* 1:17). He also noted the text as a decisive one in Galatians 3:11. In both, Paul is demonstrating the only way for men to be justified by God. Pride only shows a clinging to the essence of sin. The proud soul 'is not upright' (*Hab.* 2:4). It is 'through faith' that men become 'just' (*Hab.* 2:4). Paul explicitly states that conclusion in Romans 10:9–10: 'If you . . . believe in your heart that God has raised Him (Jesus the Lord) from the dead, you will be saved. For with the heart one believes unto righteousness . . .'

The righteousness which God declares some men to have, they receive only through faith. It is not their personal righteousness but the righteousness of another which is put to their account. Of course, his epistle triumphantly explains that 'the gift of righteousness' is 'through . . . Jesus Christ' (*Rom.* 5:1–21). 'THE LORD OUR RIGHTEOUSNESS' is his name (*Jer.* 23:6)!

Those who do not utterly rely on Christ for righteousness but rely upon their own deeds will receive the wages of their sin which is death. The *gift* of God is eternal life in Christ Jesus our Lord (*Rom.*

5:21; 6:26). Thus the great contrasts of Habakkuk are emphasized in the gospel era: pride versus faith, unrighteousness versus righteousness, and death versus life.

HABAKKUK'S PERSONAL CONTEXT

Habakkuk had sought God's reviving mercies for his nation, only to be told that a ferocious heathen empire would vandalize his people. The prophet longed for soon-to-appear blessings to his land and his temple. However, he, like saints of days long past, had to exercise faith. An expectation of immediate triumph requires less faith.

Abraham, for example, had to live most of his life without an heir, and never saw a numerous seed, though God had promised these blessings. He died, never having possessed the land of promise, nor the Seed in whom all the nations of the earth would be blessed. He who 'believed God, and it was accounted to him for righteousness' (*Gen.* 15:6) nonetheless 'waited for the city . . . whose builder and maker is God' (*Heb.* 11:10). In Abraham, and in all his spiritual children, faith was 'the conviction of things not seen' (*Heb.* 11:1). Faith embraces the written, yet unfulfilled, promises of God's words.

In Habakkuk 2:3 the man of God is told that 'the vision' (unfolding before him) 'is for an appointed time'. It contained a promise for the Jews which was not intended for immediate fulfilment. Furthermore the written vision 'strives for the end' promised. Scripture is 'living and powerful' (*Heb.* 4:13). Not only can it penetrate to man's heart, as Hebrews tells us. 'It strives after the end' (*Hab.* 2:3) of which it speaks. God's Word moves history to the results he has promised, as surely as his creative word brought our world into being.

It is to confidence in this Word that Habakkuk, and we, are called when all appearances of our day seem to move in a contrary direction. This was the faith recorded of many in Hebrews 11. It must be our faith too. We are called to a faith that is based upon the Scripture alone, not upon news reports or the sight of present fulfilments. Thus Habakkuk, and we, are told:

> Though it tarries, wait for it;
> Because it will surely come,
> It will not tarry!
>
> *Habakkuk 2:3*

Promises may seem delayed in our time, but there will be no tarrying of fulfilment in God's appointed time. Faith is always called upon to wait, rather than to have all blessings now. 'You turned to God from idols to serve the living and true God, and to wait for His Son from heaven' (*1 Thess.* 1:9–10).

Faith is not credulous, ready to latch on to every positive prediction for the future. The optimism of faith is founded upon God's character as it is revealed in his Word. We know that God can save 'by many or by few', as we were taught by Jonathan, son of Saul (*1 Sam.* 14:6). His infinite wisdom and power may reverse the fortunes of saints in a moment with little means. Our optimism is also established by precise promises in the Scriptures. Since the Lord has revealed, 'I will not totally destroy the house of Jacob' (*Amos* 5:8), we know that he never will.

There are ultimate outcomes which God has pledged. These, therefore, we believe, although all present circumstances seem to conspire against the fulfilment of divine revelation.

Because our faith (and therefore our optimism) is utterly reliant on Scripture, it must also be tempered by the same Scripture. God, in very dark times, stunningly revives true religion, so that all must admit that the event is supernatural. However, the Lord does not always do so, 'For whom the LORD loves He corrects, just as a father the son in whom he delights' (*Prov.* 3:12).

In the Scripture, God's severe correction of his sons has even come during times when there lived saints with outstanding measures of grace. Yet he did not use their gifts to revive. As Habakkuk spoke of his dread of Babylon's crushing blows to Judah, still to come, he was speaking of times in which not only he, but also Jeremiah, Daniel and Ezekiel lived. Yet their prayers and their faithful ministries were not employed in quickly accomplishing a revival that prevented severe chastisement.

We must recognize that our minds have been too caught up in a humanistic interpretation of the history of the church. Even Reformed people have succumbed to a man-centered view of revival. It is the view which suggests that if only we had a sufficiently spiritual leader doing the right things, then revival would break upon us. No! Great men of God have been called to serve in very dark hours which only became darker as they continued to be faithful. A conviction of the truth of God's promises yet unseen is great faith.

The result of a humanistic view of revival is that men point fingers at leaders during difficult times as being failures. The truth is that revival, although it comes by human means, is entirely reliant upon the divine will and power. This means that seeking revival cannot be the talk of lazy optimism. It must be the urgent pleading of the church which leads to it.

But we have to recognize also that it is not God's will to send this solution to the church's weakness in every age. We may be called upon to remain faithful in still darker times to come. We may have to 'wait' through very black eras for the bright promises to 'surely come' in God's perfect timing.

'The vision is yet for an appointed time' (*Hab.* 2:3). It is a time of the Lord's appointing.

5

God's Great Purposes
of History (2:15–17)

I N THE PROPHET'S FIRST PRAYER (*Hab.* 1:2–4), he
asked the Almighty how he could endure the
violence and injustice within Judah. God's first
revelation to his servant (1:5–11) disclosed a brutal
invasion of Judah about to come from Babylon
in response to the nation's sin. In a second prayer
(1:12–2:11) the prophet boldly questioned how a
holy God could countenance triumph by the most
wicked of men over the less wicked. We are now
considering God's second revelation to the prophet
(2:2–20).

In this answer to Habakkuk's prayer is the key to
reading all of history. A great conflict is raging on
the earth. It is the clash between the proud on one
hand and men of faith on the other. The boastful,
arrogant and self-reliant assert themselves. The righteous place all their reliance upon God. Throughout

history this Almighty God is resisting the proud but giving grace to the humble (*Hab.* 2:4). In Habakkuk 2:5–20 the Lord applies this principle to the raging bully-nation, Babylon. However, the same response from God's sovereign throne is given to every swaggering power on earth.

The God who knows all hearts described the threatening empire of Babylon in Habakkuk 2:5. The history of Babylon is characterized by its excessive use of alcohol. Human pride was propped up by means of intoxicated passion. On the night Babylon fell to the forces of Persia, all her leaders were carousing in a palace orgy. Having desires as insatiable as are death and the grave the empire heaped up captive nations and plunder from their conquests.

GOD HAS DESTINED BABYLON TO SHAMEFUL MOCKING

Of course the proud, as they always do, taunted their victims, just as the Pharisees taunted Christ on the cross. Consequently Jehovah expressed five of his own taunts to the proud Babylonians. His statements assure Habakkuk that Babylon would not have the last word in history. God would bring them to ruin after they have ruined proud Judah.

These five taunts by the living God of Providence are marked by exclamations in verses 6, 9, 12, 15, and 19. In many versions of the Bible the exclamation is translated, 'Woe.' As Dr Palmer Robertson has shown us, the word is more appropriately rendered, 'Ha!' God is mocking the mockers.

Earlier in Israel's history a giant of a warrior had stood before the Jewish forces inviting them to send out their best man to fight him. Proudly he had cried, 'I defy the armies of Israel this day.' This man of massive dimensions, wearing his mammoth armour and carrying his Herculean weapons, had stood before the Jews. A lad dressed as a shepherd had approached him. The boy had said, 'I come to you in the name of the LORD of hosts, the God of the armies of Israel, whom you have defied. This day the LORD will deliver you into my hand, and I will strike you and take your head from you.' Thus the taunter had been taunted.

Verses 6–8 bring the first taunt to Babylon and to every proud, warring oppressor in history. It is as though God points a finger and cries, '*Ha! The plunderer is plundered.*' The day is coming when the remnant of all the nations which Babylon had pillaged would rise up and pillage Babylon herself (verse 8). But God speaks not only of the spoils of military campaigns. Conquering nations also impose unjust terms of business and credit on those they oppress. Practising a policy of heavy taxation and excessive interest for loans will return to bite the proud who use these measures against others (verses 6–7).

Verses 9–11 hold God's second taunt. *'Ha! Your places of refuge have crumbled.'* Men and nations pursue 'evil gain' (verse 9) to provide protection for their houses. They are building future 'security' for their families, for their dynasties, and for their nations and empires. They are like hawks and eagles who build nests in the rocky mountainsides (verse 9b). Nevertheless, these fortresses will collapse. The proud victors will hear the rocks of their walls and the timbers of their building beams cry out against them (verse 11) as they crumble to the ground. 'Pride goes before destruction' (*Prov.* 16:18). 'The LORD will destroy the proud' (*Prov.* 15:25).

A third taunt issues from the mouth of the Lord in verses 12–14: *'Ha! Your efforts are for nothing!'* Babylon organized its people to build towns, cities, and nations. They did it with bloodshed. They did it then as nations often do now – by aiming at proud human goals. Secularism (in which man, not God, motivates their efforts) leads to the goals of materialism, hedonism, and feminism. All such building will be burned in the fires of God's judgments. It will prove to be vanity (emptiness).

Fourthly (15–17), they are told, *'Ha! You who shame others will be publicly shamed.'* Luxurious and wild entertainment at the expense of others will make you disgusting in their eyes. What you think is your glory is your dishonour. You will feel their contempt before multitudes, and in the last judgment.

GOD'S PURPOSE OF GRACE IS NOT HINDERED BY ITS ENEMIES

In the midst of this ringing indictment of the Babylonian empire, the Lord explains why all this must be so:

> For the earth will be filled with the knowledge
>   of the glory of the LORD,
> As the waters cover the sea.
>
> *Habakkuk* 2:14

God has decreed the terminal point of human history. When the tale is entirely told, everyone will see how every event and every era has served this end.

This was not the first time that God spoke these very words by the mouths of his prophets. In Numbers 14 the people of Israel had refused to enter the Promised Land as God had told them to do. They openly planned to choose a new leader to replace Moses and to lead them back to Egypt. God found it necessary to curse them with forty years of wandering in the wilderness until all the rebellious adults had died.

Yet, the Lord proclaimed on this occasion, 'Truly, as I live, all the earth shall be filled with the glory of the LORD' (*Num.* 14:21).

Also, in Isaiah 10 and 11, God had addressed the pride of Assyria with the prediction:

> Behold the Lord,
> the LORD of hosts,
> will lop off the bough with terror;
> Those of high stature will be hewn down,
> And the haughty will be humbled.
>
> *Isaiah* 10:33

With this is contrasted a branch growing out of the root of Jesse (*Isa.* 11). As the Branch (the Messiah) and his kingdom are described it is said, 'For the earth shall be full of the knowledge of the LORD as the waters cover the sea' (*Isa.* 11:9).

The supreme answer to proud humanism in all its forms is the One who said, 'I am gentle and lowly in heart' (*Matt.* 11:29). It is he of whose coming it was said:

> The glory of the Lord shall be revealed,
> and all flesh shall see it together:
> For the mouth of the Lord has spoken.
>
> *Isaiah* 40:5

Again in this place prophets were told to 'say to the cities of Judah, "Behold your God!" (*Isa.* 40:9).

THE KINGDOM OF GOD UNDER CHRIST WILL FULFIL THIS PROMISE

The New Testament tells us that the gospel of 'Christ Jesus the Lord' is a gospel of glory (2 *Cor.* 4:4). Glory speaks of splendour and greatness. And 'the glory of God' is 'in the face of Jesus Christ' (2 *Cor.* 4:6). Christ is the image of God (2 *Cor.* 4:4). He is the brightness of the Father's glory and the express image of his person (*Heb.* 1:3). The apostles testified, 'We beheld his glory, the glory as of the only begotten of the Father, full of grace and truth' (*John* 1:14).

The knowledge of this glory of God is, by God's determination, destined to cover the entire earth. It must be seen by every nation, not only by the Jews of Habakkuk's nation. In Psalm 2 God laughs at those nations in rebellion against him and his Messiah. In defiance of their will God sets his King upon Zion and promises to him the nations as an inheritance and the uttermost parts of the earth for his possession.

The god of this age (Satan) is blinding men so that they do not see the glory of God in the face of Jesus Christ (2 *Cor.* 4:4). Those who cannot see the glory are now perishing (2 *Cor.* 4:3). However, in the process of history the God who commanded light to shine out of darkness will shine on a multitude of hearts to give them the light of the knowledge of the glory of God in Christ (2 *Cor*. 4:6).

This knowledge of God's glory will fill the earth as the waters cover the sea (*Hab*. 2:14). The Jews were serving the ends of God in this purpose as they were severely chastised by the stick of Babylon. They would return to their land one day and through them would come Messiah, in whose face the glory of God would supremely and savingly shine. A great missionary movement would take the gospel of this glory to the ends of the earth. In the Messiah would be the triumph of faith over pride. Trust in God would be exalted above human self-reliance, whether intellectual or physical.

MODERN PARALLELS

Those of us who live in the West (Europe and America) have been highly privileged to have a history of our fathers' knowing the glory of God. We have further served the end of extending a knowledge of God's glory in Christ over much of the earth, 'as the waters cover the sea'. Yet there has crept into western society an 'enlightenment' which was built upon the pride of the human intellect. Such pride has been seen in the increasing challenge to all knowledge of God and his glory and in increasing attempts to diminish his significance. This advancement of pride in western man's observations and thoughts has driven faith into a corner.

The modern West is at the present time re-enacting the tragic self-destruction of the ancient classical cultures of Greece and Rome. Now, as then, universities and governments are 'suppressing the truth in unrighteousness' (*Rom.* 1:18). 'Professing to be wise', they have become 'fools' (*Rom.* 1:22). As Jesus explained, 'Everyone practising evil hates the light and does not come to the light, lest his deeds should be exposed' (*John* 3:20). Because of this hostility to truth 'God gives them up to uncleanness, in the lusts of their hearts, to dishonour their bodies among themselves' (*Rom.* 1:24). This is the first phase of 'the wrath of God' being 'revealed from heaven against all ungodliness and unrighteousness of men' (*Rom.* 1:18).

What does it look like? 'And even as they did not like to retain God in their knowledge, God gave them over to a debased mind, to do those things which are not fitting; being filled with all unrighteousness, sexual immorality, wickedness, covetousness, maliciousness; full of envy, murder, strife, deceit, evil-mindedness; they are whisperers, backbiters, haters of God, violent, proud, boasters, inventors of evil things, disobedient to parents, undiscerning, untrustworthy, unloving, unforgiving, unmerciful' (*Rom.* 1:28–31).

When moral decay eats away all strength in nations, they will fall prey to violent, evil empires. After that comes judgment at God's throne.

With this continuing trend away from faith and toward pride we live under the threat of God's chastening, as did Judah of old. If there is not serious, widespread repentance, we shall find it difficult to hide from our enemies under the shadow of God's wing.

The danger is to *us*, not to the cause of the *knowledge* of the glory of God throughout the entire earth. God stands in no need of us to give the uttermost parts of the earth to Messiah. He will accomplish his grand purpose with or without us.

It is the pride of humanism and the rejection of divine revelation which we must shake off, or God will seriously shake our nations.

6

The Ultimate Ridicule of the Proud (2:18–20)

GOD, WHO MADE HEAVEN AND EARTH and every being except himself, has a throne of dominion over all earthly governments and their history. From this throne the Almighty does according to his will, casting down the proud and exalting the humble.

Under his sovereign rule the only true God even makes use of arrogant and violent nations to punish other earthly societies immersed in the defiance of his holy laws. Yet any nation which lives by pride and not by humble faith will be hurled down to ruin when the King of heaven has finished using it. In this manner when a boastful ruler and nation come under the wrath of God, they are exposed as being foolish.

One of the most pompous nations of history was Babylon. Its army raged against the Lord and his Messiah. Yet, it pleased God to employ Babylon to give severe correction to a wayward Judah along with other depraved societies. Even as Babylon was merely beginning to take counsel against the Lord and against his Anointed, the Lord who sat in the heavens laughed at them. Mocking taunts in rapid succession were hurled from God's mouth to this wicked nation (*Hab.* 2:4–19). There is always complete certainty that the proud (both individuals and nations) will fail to succeed in their evil purposes, except insofar as God is using them for his own righteous ends.

THE EVILS OF FALSE RELIGION

Habakkuk 2:18–20 demonstrates for us what the pinnacle of our Lord's derision of the proud always is. God's ridicule of Babylon had gradually risen in tone (through verses 6, 7, 9, 12, and 15). Now the crescendo of mockery breaks upon the brazen in verses 18 and 19. Here Jehovah lampoons the proud man of all ages for the silliest, the most senseless element of his errant ways:

There is no fear of God before his eyes (*Psa.* 36:13).

The nation of Judah fell under the whip of Babylon because its citizens had turned their backs on the only true God and had followed false religions in the worship of idols. Now Babylon itself would be destroyed for its own worship of idols. On the night that Darius the Mede captured Babylon and killed Belshazzar, ruler of the kingdom and son of Nebuchadnezzar, the king and his nobles had been drinking from goblets taken from Judah at the sacking of the Temple in Jerusalem. A hand, writing on the wall, supernaturally appeared to the revellers.

The by-now-forgotten Daniel was called to explain this frightening vision. God's prophet reminded Belshazzar that his father had 'acknowledged that the Most High God is sovereign over the kingdoms of men and sets over them anyone he wishes' (*Dan.* 5:21). Then he added, 'But you his son have not humbled yourself, though you knew all this. Instead, you have set yourself up against the Lord of heaven . . . You praised the gods of silver and gold, of bronze, iron, wood and stone, which cannot see or hear or understand. But you did not honour *the God who holds in his hand your life and all your ways*' (verse 22).

The first four of Moses' Ten Commandments have to do with:

1. Whom we worship.
2. How we worship him.
3. The reverence with which we must use his name.

4.   What time we must devote to him.

This matter of the fear and worship of the one true God is placed first and is spoken of at greater length than the remaining six commands because it is the most vital element of morality.

Without the existence of a fear of God the remaining commandments will not be established in the life either of a person or of a nation. Sin against God, our Maker and Judge, is far more serious than sin against man. Offences toward men are so wrong because all mankind is made in the image of God. Therefore keeping the last six commands is 'like unto' keeping the first four.

Judgment falls on proud men and nations because they hold God in contempt and devote themselves to false religion. From the earliest days of human life on earth men have invented systems of religion to rival the worship stipulated by the true and living God.

While Abel humbly followed divinely-given directives for worship, Cain proudly invented another scheme which seemed to him superior to the one dictated by God's words. Later on, shortly after Noah, Shem, Ham, and Japheth had exited the ark, humanity was worshipping a plethora of gods by means of carved or graven images. Improper worship of the true God and worship of false gods has long involved the use of idols.

The Ultimate Ridicule of the Proud (2:18–20)

When God told Babylon (and all the proud) that their gods and their worship were useless, he was directing attention to the most absurd aspect of human thought and behaviour. 'What profit is the image?' (*Hab.* 2:18a).

This plain statement of God Most High should strike confusion into the hearts of all who claim to worship the God of the Bible, but who continue to show reverence to images made by man. Even beyond this the one true and living God is emphasizing the utter futility of *all* humanly-imagined deities and religions. Temporal judgments are dispatched by God for just such sins.

Nations of the West have had fathers in their families and national fathers among their rulers who bowed the knee to the God of Scripture. However, it has become the generally accepted opinion of western nations that equal respect must be shown to all religions. The 'Enlightenment' brought about opposition to the first four commandments. The modern invention of 'toleration', or of giving equal status to all gods and all religions, is nonsense. There is no profit to images or to the religious systems which produced them. Yet modern westerners feel themselves noble and honourable for contradicting this foundational declaration of God's Word.

Images teach lies! 'The moulded image, a teacher of lies' (verse 18b). These images are made by men.

How, then, can men turn round and put trust in the work of their own hands? There is neither breath nor life in images. How can they help those who worship them? How can they arise and deliver those who pray to them? Images only mislead.

GOD, OUR CREATOR

The God of the Bible is our Maker! He is worthy of trust. He is a Spirit who created all that exists apart from himself. Therefore he has power over all creation.

Do not mistake the importance of the Enlightenment's denial of the biblical teaching of creation. That (evolutionary) principle of modern faith represents a human philosophical (not scientific) effort to destroy faith in the Creator of heaven and earth. It is an attempt to reduce the God of Scripture to the level of all man-made idols. Indeed, the reasonings of so-called 'enlightened' man are pure speculations that creation is a falsehood invented by the human mind. He views the doctrine of creation as being similar to the attempts by artists to create a god of their own imaginations.

GOD HAS SPOKEN

As idols are created, not creators, they are also 'mute' (verse 18). They do not speak to those who worship them. False religions are filled with religious ideas and words. However, all of these words and thoughts originate with men. Our God has spoken in human language and has recorded his words for us in Holy Scripture. But liberalism and neo-orthodoxy, in keeping with the teachings of the Enlightenment, go to great lengths to turn the Bible into the mere words of men about God.

Denying God's creative work and his revelation in human words has been carried out by massive labours on the part of those who proclaim the thoughts of the Enlightenment. If all religions are reduced to one level, it becomes perfectly clear that none of them is of much use. If the God of the Bible can be shrunk so as to fit into the category of idols, neither creating nor speaking, but invented by men, he will be of no more profit than are the most base forms of religion ever to be found.

All of these continuing assaults upon God by the 'enlightenment' of western society are aimed at turning man's trust from God and turning man's ear away from listening to God's words. To the extent that enlightenment proclamations have succeeded in our educational institutions and governments, they have led to an ever-loftier pride within man. Man's mind is now his own object of trust. For instance, the minds of professors in universities, our own minds, and our scientific outlook are considered supreme. Educators, legislators, and scientists are in the business of setting themselves up as having the final word. They are labouring to win for themselves the faith which is due to God alone. It is all to no profit. For there is a God with breath; there *is* a God who produces words. *His* words create and destroy. *His* words show the way to life in this world and the next. *His* words bring all men into final judgment.

The answer to the scheme of western thought is the assertion of Habakkuk 2:20:

> The LORD *is* in His holy temple.
> Let all the earth keep silence before Him!

All of the babble of men on these subjects, whether they be scholars, rulers, or priests, is impertinent and silly. The reality of the existence of God in his heavenly temple, described in Isaiah 6, Hebrews 12, and Revelation 4 and 5, compels all proud human inventors of worship to be silent before the Creator of all things and the Revealer of all truth.

Secular neutrality is an abandonment of all morality. Secular men in the West presume that they can eliminate religion from practical life and from state decisions. Yet, the wars thrust upon us are of a religious nature. Historically, when Roman Catholics and Protestants ceased facing off their armies in Europe, there was soon a Napoleon attempting to impose the scepticism of the French Revolution on other nations. More recently the fanatical religion of Hitler and yet another one in Japan forced many nations into a world-wide war. Today as then anti-Semitism is roiling among Muslim nations where *Mein Kampf* is popular reading. Military Islam is professedly anti-Jewish and anti-Christian.

SILENCE BEFORE GOD

To the aggressively proud, God says, 'Be still and know that I am God':

As if to say, 'I am not like your idol-gods, moulded by your human hands for your own convenience. I made you and shape who you are and where your life will end. I am not silent but have spoken. By my words life is given to man, and only by my word will he have eternal life. Silence your opposition to me!'

To the agitated believer God says, 'Be still and know that I am God':

As if to say, 'I hold in my hand all enemies who threaten you. Although they may do my will, they will never destroy my people! I place my servants (Joseph, Mordecai, Daniel, and Nehemiah) in the most powerful positions within heathen governments to preserve my people. I send angels to keep her enemies from obliterating my people in the most destructive assaults (*Ezek.* 9). The gates of Hell will not destroy Christ's Church (*Matt.* 16:18). In the same way no one has erased the Jewish people from this earth, although many have intended genocide against them. Silence your fears!'

The infinite distance between the dignity of God and that of all his creatures demands reverent silence before him. He does speak, and we are to listen. On the Mount of Transfiguration, God displayed the glory of Christ with unique vividness. In response Peter began to blurt out his ideas of activity and words of admiration for all that he saw. A Voice from heaven interrupted him and said, 'This is My beloved Son, in whom I am well pleased. Hear Him!' (*Matt.* 17:5). Listen to Him! Keep quiet before Him! When God is near and disclosing his own glory a holy hush falls over assemblies of men, the power of which is felt by even the small children present.

So much of modern worship, which calls itself 'Christian', displays a nervousness to fill every moment 'in church' with human doings, human speaking, and human singing. But our God with breath has spoken. At last he has spoken in his Son. Listen to him!

Quiet your hearts, look to him in reverence, and let his words be the dominant element of your worship! Not *your* words, but *his*, are of supreme importance.

7

Habakkuk's Third Prayer (3:1–19)

CHAPTER THREE OF OUR PROPHETIC BOOK contains the final recorded prayer of this man of God. No answer of Jehovah to this prayer is given. In effect chapter three is Jehovah's answer to the two previous prayers. The answer is not spoken by the Lord, but the answer is worked into the heart and words of Habakkuk.

Yet the third prayer is not merely a spiritual exercise of one man of God, as were the former two. This prayer is intended for public use as is shown by verse 1: 'A prayer of Habakkuk the prophet, on Shigionoth', and by verse 19: 'To the Chief Musician. With my stringed instruments.'

This prayer would be sung by faithful Jews in the temple at Jerusalem as the Babylonian terror approached. It would be sung by faithful oppressed Jews in exile. It would be sung after the restoration.

PREPARATION FOR THE PRAYER

The final verbal answer from Jehovah to the Praying Prophet is found in Habakkuk 2:20:

> The LORD is in His holy temple.
> Let all the earth keep silence before Him.

The Almighty dwells in his temple. That temple is the place of God's worship, but it also serves as a throne room (the seat of government) for the Father and the Son! (Note the composite throne room–temple in Isaiah 6, and in Revelation 5, 6 and 21:22).

Habakkuk's first two prayers were composed of agitated complaints to the Most High. The first was a complaint against Jehovah for his delay in putting an end to immorality and injustice in Judah. The second was a complaint against Jehovah for his intent to use a nation still more wicked than they to chastise Judah for her sins. Are not many of our most fervent prayers just that – complaints against our Sovereign? Is it not true that we dare to cast aspersions on the One who rules over us, over our churches, over our nations, and over the world today?

When we are irritated with the Lord for the manner in which he governs the affairs of our times we have one need above all others. It is to have a view of the Judge of all the earth in his sheer majesty and supreme competence. He is in his holy temple. The required consequence of such a vision is spoken. 'Let all the earth hush before Him.' God spoke to Habakkuk as a father speaks to a vexed child, 'Hush!' The firm hand of the Father is sufficient to change the child's tone. There were no more complaints against God from Habakkuk. There should be no hint of grumbling from us. There was none in the prayer of Habakkuk 3.

'But', we sputter, 'we are in a very dangerous emergency!' 'Hush, child!' are the Father's sufficient words. When Jeremiah lived to witness the crushing of Jerusalem by Babylon he came to a similar conclusion in his Lamentations: 'It is good that one should hope and wait quietly for the salvation of the LORD' (*Lam.* 3:26)! The faith of which Habakkuk wrote (*Hab.* 2:4), the faith which makes men just and brings them life, is a faith which often suffers and often lives through calamities. It was the quiet faith of the believing Jews in captivity.

Today some Evangelicals have noisy meetings to drum up victory. Others shout in political rallies to 'make a difference' and change the ways of nations. 'Let all the earth hush before Him.' Acquiesce in the decrees of the Holy One. Lean upon the Lord in the midst of adversity; it is good for refining the grace of hope (Read Calvin's commentary on Lamentations 3:24–26, on quietness in adversity – see *Appendix*).

AN ESSENTIAL INGREDIENT IN PRAYER

The actual prayer began, 'O LORD, I have heard Your speech and was afraid.' Jehovah had spoken to Habakkuk in human words in response to his first two prayers. The prophet had heard and considered what the Almighty had said. Both replies had expressed God's perfect holiness. The Most High is so morally upright that he had announced his anger first against a lawbreaking Judah and then against a thoroughly corrupt and wicked Babylon. God's anger against sin arises from his own flawless character. The Scriptures speak of God's anger as 'burning' and 'smoking.' Note that God's wrath is without partiality.

In his righteous fury the Lord judges all and executes his sentences against both Israel and her atoning sacrifice. But because the heathen have no acceptable sacrifice the Lord's kindled wrath consumes them forever. Habakkuk appropriately responded to the divine threats of coming judgments – with fear. It would be proper to translate the Hebrew term for fear as 'trembling.' In Isaiah 66:2 God describes the one on whom he will look:

> On him who is poor and of a contrite spirit
> And who trembles at My word.

Trembling before the Word of God is a part of the experience of becoming meek before him. Only through awareness of our personal sins against God and of our just deserving of his angry curse are we ready to turn to the Saviour for pardon and grace. Trembling is the pathway to mercy and stillness before our Maker. Listen and be afraid!

PLEADING FOR MERCY

No longer does Habakkuk argue against God's purposes to crush Judah in the near future. No longer is he horrified that a most depraved nation will be the Lord's instrument for Judah's judgment.

Accepting and trembling at the most unpleasant prospects, the quieted prophet sought to pray appropriately. He realized that he must no longer insist that his own plan direct God's providence. Righteousness will not come to his nation by means of a soft landing. Nor will God annihilate the most vicious idol worshipers before they can injure his chosen people.

Yet God's revelation has opened a window of prayer for the burdened prophet. This window is the grand promise given to Habakkuk, one of the key promises of all the Bible:

> The just shall live by his faith.
> *Habakkuk* 2:4

Thus Habakkuk and all believing Jews had legitimate requests to make. For, after all, 'Prayer is

asking God for things which he has promised to give'
(*Children's Catechism*). Twice Habakkuk framed the
public prayer in terms of the phrase, 'In the midst
of the years'. Commentators dispute whether this
phrase has an eschatological sense. But surely it
means, 'In the midst of the years' of Judah's destruction, and 'in the midst of the years' of her captivity;
'in the midst of the years' of Babylon's terrorizing
raids and her oppressive powers, and 'in the midst
of the years' of our own great tribulations.'

MAKE HIM LIVE

'In the midst of the years make him live' (verse 2)!
Make who live? The man of faith! Make his soul
alive in you, and let him live through the gathering
storm of disaster. No, the saints do not escape the
horrors and sadnesses of their nations' judgments
from the hand of God. But through steadfast faith
they live! God can keep their hearts alive in faith
and even preserve their lives in the midst of general
slaughters.

MAKE HIM UNDERSTAND

'In the midst of the years make him understand'
(verse 2)! In peace and safety we line up our doctrines
and feel secure. But there comes a new requirement
of deep understanding of the ways of God when

men are swept up in the tragedies and disasters of their nations which have forsaken God and despised his law.

REMEMBER MERCY

'In trembling remember mercy' (verse 2)! As the time of judgment approaches Habakkuk envisions himself and all true believers as trembling. The wicked may curse God, but they will not tremble before him. The wicked may fear earthly means of destruction, but not the God who lifts the rod which directs these means. But those who tremble before a holy, angry and just God – the ultimate source of judgment – will appeal to him for mercy. Deserving no relief from God's smoking justice, men and women of faith realize that there is pardon for sin in Jesus Christ, God's Son and God's Lamb of sacrifice. At the very time of wrath there is mercy to be shown to those who have faith.

THE PRAYERS ANSWERED

This pleading that those of faith would be made alive by divine action was God's means of preserving lives through the most alarming times. In 606 BC, when Nebuchadnezzar first conquered Jerusalem, Daniel, Shadrach, Meshach, and Abednego lived through the holocaust.

Scripture records that, even in captivity, their living faith was dramatically displayed to Nebuchadnezzar himself and to his nation. The prayer, based on the promise of Habakkuk 2, that they might 'understand', led to there being divine prophecy and the gifts of wisdom among the Jews, even in their darkest hours.

During Nebuchadnezzar's second conquest of Jerusalem, Ezekiel, a man of great faith, was preserved alive. His living prophecies to the Jews in exile are recorded in the Old Testament book which bears his name. While in Babylon he prophesied of God's giving a new heart to his people Israel. And he understood and taught that God must be inquired of according to his promises to do for them what he has promised (*Ezek.* 36:37).

In 536 BC, in answer to Daniel's prayer (*Dan.* 9), men of faith (Zerubbabel, Joshua, and Haggai) led the first contingent of exiles back to Jerusalem. In 458 BC, Ezra led a second group back. In 445 BC, Nehemiah came to aid in the restoration. Men of faith lived through the most fearsome events and gave vitality to the body of God's people. They outlived their heathen conquerors and the cruel nations that oppressed them.

All the while the bright beam of righteousness and truth burned through further lights who continued to live in exile, such lights as Mordecai and Esther.

God was pouring out mercy in the midst of very frightening years.

If the modern church should live through well-deserved national calamities under the wrath of God the Lord is able to let his people live, to let them understand and to taste mercy. Ezekiel 9 tells us how God preserves his special people even during scenes of the most general slaughter. For example, Ezekiel was prophesying in exile during the third and most horrific conquest of Jerusalem by Nebuchadnezzar. Life, understanding, and mercy abounded to his saints even in this, one of the kind of scenes throughout history which make all knees to tremble.

If God destroyed a wicked world in Noah's day, if he eradicated Sodom and Gomorrah, if Jehovah sent his special people into exile and reproach among the nations, will he spare modern western nations, once 'Christian', who repeat the same sins? Here is a prayer to keep in the pocket of your memory for those dark hours of judgment.

Acquaint yourself with mercy in Christ, and be certain that you enter the upheavals of war, conquest, and oppression as a person of steadfast faith. Men and women of faith shine as jewels of mercy amidst the deepest gloom of sin and unbelief. Because they are products of divine mercy, God is greatly glorified in them and by them, even when other types of triumph do not appear.

8

Spectators of Divine Majesty (3:3–16)

CHAPTER THREE OF HABAKKUK is the great temple prayer composed by the prophet against the backdrop of God's revelations to him in chapters one and two. These had predicted two great historic crises, one for Judah under attack from Babylon and one for Babylon in the day of her destruction. Habakkuk's prayer began with petitions in verses 1 and 2. He pleaded for believers in Israel — that God would grant them life, understanding and mercy in the midst of the critical years. However, prayer to God is composed of more than making requests of the Most High.

A UNIQUE FEATURE OF HUMAN NATURE

Have you ever contemplated the strange aspect of human experience which we share only with angels in the array of the living creatures of God? Man is by nature a spectator. We all watch and enter into the exploits of others. In the competitions of sport we delight in observing an athlete's skill. If our champion wins a contest we share the satisfaction of his highest displays of talent, and we feel that we have won along with him. There are immediate shouts of triumph at his winning, but then countless hours and efforts of rehearsing his exploits naturally follow.

There are the same enjoyment of and union with skilled musicians at concerts. One or a few produce the music, but thousands may be united with them in spirit as they perform. Giving a speech or preaching a sermon may be much the same. One speaks, but many more may be carried along in the unique experience of the oratory. We are then spectators, deriving emotional, intellectual and very real experiences from others. Their thrills in success and tragedies of defeat become our very own. Of course this argues that we are spiritual beings.

SPECIALLY SUITED TO OUR CENTRAL PLACE IN GOD'S PURPOSES

Above all we were made to be spectators of divine majesty. We were formed to glorify God and to enjoy him forever. Much of this is done through prayer! With an eye cast upon the mighty works of

God, we are to rehearse his greatness from hearts that have entered into his glorious feats. To describe heartily his doings is the essence of praise. Habakkuk had just learned of two of the coming great acts of God. These were not disclosed merely to satisfy his curiosity. The revelation is intended to draw God's spectators into support of his execution of these great deeds.[1]

How does God appear when he comes 'for the salvation of Your people, for salvation with Your anointed' (verse 13)? 'His glory covers the heavens, and His praise fills the earth. And His brilliance is as the light' (*Hab.* 3:3–4). The dominant impression made when God arises to save is glory, splendour, majesty, shining excellence, light and beauty.

When Jesus came to save his people from their sins he was 'the brightness of His Father's glory and the express image of His person' (*Heb.* 1:3). 'The glory of God [was] in the face of Jesus Christ' (2 *Cor.* 4:6). John was correct to describe his coming as 'the light shines in darkness' (*John* 1:5). However, so blind were men to that light that God sent John the Baptist just to tell them that the light was

---

[1] To study the Hebrew words and Hebrew poetic structure in this passage, consult the excellent work by O. Palmer Robertson, *The Books of Nahum, Habakkuk, and Zephaniah* (1990), in the *New International Commentary on the Old Testament*, published by Eerdmans

shining. Yet later, for all the apostles, the apostle John said, 'We beheld His glory, the glory as of the only begotten of the Father, full of grace and truth' (*John* 1:14). All believing observers of salvation must sing of the glory of the divine presence which acts. Satan actively labours to blind the eyes of men lest they be spectators of God's excellent greatness (2 *Cor.* 4:4).

As part of telling of the glory of the Holy One, Habakkuk extensively described his power. 'Horns [symbols of strength] flash from His hand, and there His power is hidden' (*Hab.* 3:4b). Omnipotence will be displayed in God's salvation. The force of the Almighty leaves man with no descriptive analogies. It is hidden, immeasurable and beyond man's knowing. Our Saviour-God is worthy of everlasting praises, thundering praises, for he is the only potentate. None can withstand his power.

RECOGNITION OF DIVINE POWER

In this poetic prayer Habakkuk enabled the saints of his day to foresee certain events. As worshippers watch and enjoy God's saving work, it is not altogether a pleasing scene. The Holy One will save a remnant in Israel. He will be merciful to them. By his grace they will live and be righteous in his sight through faith. The unbelieving and disobedient in Israel will at the same time be destroyed. He who is

Saviour and Lord of the church is also Lord of all the nations. Nations hostile to his truth and righteousness will be crushed even as God is merciful to those who have faith. He will 'break them with a rod of iron' and 'dash them to pieces like a potter's vessel' (*Psa.* 2:9).

As God comes (to save), 'Before Him goes a plague and a burning pestilence at His feet' (*Hab.* 3:5). The Lord advances with frightening consequences to men and demons who are his malignant enemies. When Israel was brought out of Egypt plagues struck all the Egyptians (terrible plagues, such as all their first-born sons dying in one night). When the horses and riders pursued Israel they were cast into the sea. Likewise Jesus, who came to save his people from their sins, also came to 'destroy the works of the devil' (*1 John* 3:8). The very same God who ensured that the gospel would be sent out into all the earth was at the same time causing Jerusalem to be destroyed by her enemies. Later, Rome (and all worldwide empire) was crushed. No worldwide empire has since dominated the earth, though many sinister nations have attempted to do so. In Christ's last acts to save his people he and his forces will leave behind the greatest carnage of all time (*Rev.* 19).

Liberalism, both old and new, has attempted to remove all wrath and vengeance from the true God.

This movement recognizes the fierce anger of God against sin in the Old Testament. Yet its adherents teach that the God of the New Testament differs from this Old Testament view of God. They teach that God is now all mercy and kindness. To do so it is necessary to rewrite the New Testament, which liberals are delighted to do. To scrub the gospel clean (to their way of thinking) they choose some biblical themes and ignore others.

Are you ashamed of God's anger toward sinners or of his visiting just punishments upon them? Then what will you make of the cross of our Lord Jesus Christ whom the New Testament describes in Old Testament language as 'the Lamb of God who takes away the sin of the world' (*John* 1:29)? The cross is not explained merely by Judas, the Chief Priests, the Pharisees and the Roman authorities. The cross is a display of God's making his own sinless Son 'to be sin for us so that we might be made the righteousness of God in him' (2 *Cor.* 5:21). God comes in frightening majesty when he comes to be merciful to his people.

Arriving at his intended destination, the Holy One 'stands' and 'looks' (*Hab.* 3:6a). His look is taking measure of the earth. This look also startles the nations, both the nation of Israel and heathen nations. All are terrified at the presence of the Lord. Men do well to be weak-kneed. Events of cosmic proportions are about to occur. Actions of epic dimensions will be accomplished.

'The everlasting mountains are shattered. The perpetual hills bow before Him' (*Hab.* 3:6b). All this is in response to 'a look'. What will men do when he uncovers the powers hidden in his hand to strike them?

This section of Habakkuk's prayer ends with reference to the tents of two of Israel's earliest enemies. Both were tent-dwellers. Bible readers especially recall the collapse of the tents of Midian in the days of Gideon (*Judg.* 7). Habakkuk refers to the trembling of Midian's tents when the Holy One 'stood' still and 'looked'. Fear made their dwellings to shake (*Hab.* 3:7).

All of the actions of God are the believers' triumphs. That is true whether the One whose 'ways are everlasting' attacks traitors and rebels in the midst of God's people or whether he attacks our inveterate enemies who are outside of his church. Habakkuk and the Jews of his day expected successive destruction, in Israel first and later of Babylon. In each case the result would be salvation and life to those of faith (*Hab.* 2:4).

Christians in the western world have witnessed massive defections from the truths of the Bible over the last century and a quarter. Although some revival of belief in the truth did come during the last fifty years, moral and spiritual decay continue to exercise their evil effects in our nations. Our new 'Reformation' has not produced widespread conversions to Christ at this time. Will the Holy One come to our lands with fearful chastisings? Will these precede a return to the Lord and his Word? Whatever the case, *Christ will build his church!* Whatever the case, individuals with true faith will live. When the Lord comes in glory and power, when he stands with piercing gaze unsettling his enemies, we ought to follow Habakkuk's example.

It is ours to observe the glory, and to sing of his might. It is ours to celebrate cosmic disruptions arranged by his purposes (cf. 2 *Pet.* 3). It is ours to believe, live, understand and enter into the Lord's works with praise. Men never change the course of history, but believers are *there* when God does so. They triumph in him!

FACING TWO WAYS

With verses 8–16, the temple hymn turns to a direct address of the Saviour-God. The second person singular 'you' is used to speak to him. No longer are the singers merely surveying the scene of God's mighty works. Now they salute the Mighty Worker personally.

The issue of deliverance in mercy takes up the imagery of past salvation. Yet similar events must occur in the future as the Lord answers the plea, 'In wrath remember mercy.' Only the Creator can employ the great forces of the universe in his exploits. He calls rivers and seas to fight for him (verses 8 and 10). These lines recall the triumphs at the Red Sea and the Jordan River. But final bowls of wrath will yet fall upon the waters of the earth. Sun and moon stand still while the Almighty executes his wrath and brings deliverance (*Hab.* 3:11; *Josh.* 10:12–13). Mountains tremble (*Hab.* 3:10).

With creation summoned to assist his cause, Jehovah rides on horses and chariots as a Warrior. He carries glittering spear and arrows dedicated to slaying the wicked (*Hab.* 3:9, 11). With 'indignation' (verse 12) he goes forth for the salvation of his people *and* the trampling of nations.

It is exactly because God would invade Israel at the head of the Babylonian army that Habakkuk trembled in his body with quivering lips and rottenness in his bones (*Hab.* 3:16). All he could do was to wait submissively for the divinely-appointed invasion of Israel. The prophet told Jehovah that he awaited the event with quiet trembling. There was no other suitable salvation for the faithful along with destruction of the wicked but the Lord's perfect plan.

Would God call us to await such terrifying providences in our lands, where faith and its attendant righteousness are so low? Can we worship as the divine plan of history unfolds? Can we be still as we tremble in expectation?

9

Habakkuk: A Book for Times of Extreme Crisis (3:17–19)

ABAKKUK ASKED GOD to remove wickedness and injustice from a nation that professed to believe in the High and Holy One who inhabits eternity. He was told of God's purpose to chastise this wayward people severely. The rod with which the Lord would correct them would be a violent invasion by a cruel and bloodthirsty enemy. The aggressors would destroy the 'land' which God had given Israel and would carry large portions of the Jewish population into captivity.

When it became certain to the prophet that there would be no escaping the ferocity of the Babylonian enemy his entire being trembled:

> I hear, and my body trembles;
> My lips quiver at the sound;

Rottenness enters into my bones;
My legs tremble beneath me . . .
Habakkuk 3:16

This ancient saint fully shared the weakness of human flesh, experiencing to the depths fear in the face of extremity.

The people of God often cannot escape the coming to pass of their greatest fears in this life. It may be national collapse as they are vandalized by conquering enemies. It may be death at the stake for those most prominent in declaring the unwelcome gospel. It may be a very personal struggle that is lost when seeking to escape the long-felt pains of dreaded incurable disease. Some are called upon to come to death in many unwanted circumstances.

RECOGNITION OF COMING LOSS

In prayer Habakkuk's imagination ran to the survey of consequences from the coming brutal invasion of the land by Babylon. Like a horde of locusts the heathen army would strip Israel of its beauty, productivity and pleasure:

The fig tree would not bud.
No fruit would appear on grape vines.
Olive trees would bear no crop.
From the fields would come no grain.
Flocks would be cut off.

> Stalls would stand empty,
>> having no herd to inhabit them.
>>> From *Habakkuk* 3:17

The army of Nebuchadnezzar would consume all that supports life, leaving behind a hungry nation, a broken economy and an unproductive, barren landscape. Fruitfulness of the earth, the sign of God's blessing and the joy of Israel, would disappear.

This is not an unrealistic description of a region over which there have been major military operations. War and oppressive government bring about more famine than do natural conditions. Jeremiah was not the only prophet to lament Jerusalem's fall. The sad moan of grief is well expressed in Habakkuk 3:17.

JOY IN GOD DURING TIMES OF DEEPEST PRIVATION

In his struggle with God in prayer about revealed future events the great prophet came to an inward resolution of his discontent.

Man is *like* the beasts of the earth. We do have bodies, ours having been made of the dust of the ground, which crave material sustenance. Physically we need the fruits of the earth and animal products to live. Yet humans are *unlike* the other earthly creatures. God breathed into us living souls. While we do have common *physical* interests with the animal kingdom, we have a much higher community of welfare with spiritual realities and beings.

It is this fact which Jesus had in view when, during hours of intense hunger from lack of nourishment for his body, he told Satan, 'Man shall not live by bread alone, but by every word that comes from the mouth of God' (*Matt.* 4:4). Again our Saviour spoke of spiritual nourishment when he told his disciples, 'I have food to eat that you do not know about' (*John* 4:32). In like fashion, when Habakkuk sees – for he was a 'seer' (*Hab.* 1:1) – the land stripped of all that nourishes the body, he exclaims:

> Yet I will rejoice in the LORD;
> I will take joy in the God of my salvation.
> *Habakkuk* 3:18

This is the conclusion of one thought, which includes verse 17 above. He began, '*Although*' the land is stripped of all that brings the body subsistence, '*yet*' I will have joy in God. There is great satisfaction for God's people to find in God himself in times of severe want. It is sad that Christians too seldom fast. One of the lessons of fasting is that when the body is denied its pleasures, spiritual satisfactions in God alone may increase greatly. When the material world lures us to intemperance and luxury, it is so easy to forget the Lord, neglect communion with him and fail to depend on him alone. In the modern western nations, religion has commonly been turned into a quest for material things: the healing of the body, economic prosperity, etc. Did not Jeremiah say, to the contrary, 'You shall seek me and find me when you seek me with all your heart' (*Jer.* 29:13)?

When Jesus gave bread miraculously to thousands (*John* 6), crowds swarmed around our Lord looking for more bread. Christ rebuked them for not seeking *him* who is the bread of life.

Habakkuk is meditating in the spirit of Romans 8:35–37. Nothing can separate us from the love of God in Christ – not tribulation, persecution, famine or sword. Paul then says, 'In all these things we are more than conquerors through him who loved us' (verse 37). The apostle does not say that we shall never pass through extreme material and physical deprivation. On the contrary, he says that in all these circumstances of suffering loss we continue to possess the love of our God.

As we read the concluding words of the prophet Habakkuk, we perceive that there are haunting questions for all of us. Is the Lord your portion and your delight? Do you find earthly delicacies tasteless when the Lord has withdrawn the light of his countenance ('When Jesus no longer I see')?[1] Are food in

---

[1] How tedious and tasteless the hours
When Jesus no longer I see,
Sweet prospects, sweet birds, and sweet flowers
Have lost all their sweetness with me . . .
JOHN NEWTON, *Olney Hymns*, 46.

the pantry and money in the bank account your true props? Or do you lean upon the Lord?

You must learn to rejoice in the Lord! All the sweet material things of earth will forsake you. A day will come when you must say goodbye to all of earth's pleasures. You will have to say farewell to friends on the earth. Through faith God will be sweetest in the hours of bitterest partings from earthly joys. '*All* flesh is grass and *all* its glory like the flower of grass. The grass withers and the flower falls, but the word of the Lord remains for ever' (*1 Pet.* 1:24–25). What are you clutching to your heart? Is it something you cannot hold? Or is it God and his promises?

From this portion of his book, we know that, if he remained alive at the invasion of Babylon and its aftermath, Habakkuk had already learned that he would nonetheless have 'joy in the God of his salvation'. No enemy or circumstance could deprive him, and none can rob any saint of joy in God.

A CELEBRATION OF TRIUMPH

Having called Jehovah 'the God of my salvation' (verse 18), the prophet boasts in the ultimate triumph that the Lord will give him. The poetry of verse 19 is in reality the language of war.

'*He makes my feet like the deer's.*' God enables his people to move swiftly and deftly through earth's tribulations. As the deer, darting through the forest, neither crashes into trees nor slips on rocks so shall the believer remain unharmed in the face of earth's emergencies, and of death itself. Though hunted by Satan or stalked by the world and our own flesh we run our course by faith.

We are running amid the arrows of this life, some very poisonous. However, because of 'the feet of deer' which God has given us we always evade the final, fatal blow. How did Israel survive the successive brutalities of Babylon, of Persia, of Greece, and of Rome? For millennia true faith has survived on earth – only God knows how. The saints came safely to their appointed rest. All have had the gift of 'feet like the deer's'.

Another line of triumph in the poem is, *'He makes me tread on my high places.'* It is astounding that Habakkuk felt this truth in the hours of the impending disasters of war. To tread upon high places is the privilege of victors. Warriors would run along the highest ridges overlooking the valleys in which their battles had been won. Later they would ride chariots along the heights. It was very similar to the victory lap in an Olympic race. All this was done to demonstrate their dominance over what lay below them.

No revelation is given of the final state of the Jewish religion in this book. We read no specifics of the hour of triumph. Yet it is our awareness that there is such an hour that enables us to face our most alarming and dangerous circumstances along the narrow road that leads to life. '*In* all these things we are *more than conquerors*' (*Rom.* 8:37). *More* than conquerors! It is 'through him who loved us'. It is from this personal embrace of God's love that nothing whatever can separate us. 'Thanks be to God, who gives us the victory through our Lord Jesus Christ' (*1 Cor.* 15:16).

This last verse is written in view of our resurrection which is to follow death when the Lord Jesus comes again.

Our souls are anchored on these certainties. The truth is that our Saviour triumphed on the other side of a horrid death on the cross. We have not been promised that we would never suffer as he did. On the contrary, we are explicitly told that the servant is as his master. But beyond *any* injury we bear for the moment, we shall rise with him and share a glorious new heaven and new earth with him.

Do all of these words of the prophet trouble you? Is the reality of God's fellowship no source of joy and sustenance in dark hours? Can you face even the ravages of war and be certain of final triumph? Have you faced the deepest realities of God who is Spirit and of your need of spiritual renovation in Christ?

A Book for Times of Extreme Crisis (3:17–19)

Do you know of the highest joys and most secure blessings in Christ through the forgiveness of your sins? Have you a hope beyond your home and travels and present friends? Where are you going? For what are you living?

Ponder the great statement of faith in Habakkuk 3:17–19. This is faith in an hour of adversity. And the Bible's great theme is stated in Habakkuk 2:4, 'The righteous shall live by his faith.'

Call on the Lord Jesus for mercy in the face of your sins. Ask him for everlasting life. Only in him is this triumph of which Habakkuk spoke.

Appendix

Calvin on Quietness in Adversity[1]

> The LORD is my portion, saith my soul; therefore
> will I hope in him (*Lam.* 3:24).

THE PROPHET INTIMATES IN THIS VERSE that we cannot stand firm in adversities, except we be content with God alone and his favour; for as soon as we depart from him, any adversity that may happen to us will cause our faith to fail. It is then the only true foundation of patience and hope to trust in God alone; and this is the case when we are persuaded that his favour is sufficient for our perfect safety. In this sense it is that David calls God his portion (*Psa.* 16:5). But there is in the words an

[1] Extracts from John Calvin: *Commentary on Jeremiah and Lamentations* (1559, 1855; reprinted Edinburgh: Banner of Truth, 1989), vol. 5, pp. 408–13. See p. 67 of the present book.

implied contrast, for most men seek their happiness apart from God. All desire to be happy, but as the thoughts of men wander here and there, there is nothing more difficult than so to fix all our hopes in God as to disregard all other things . . .

That we may not then fail in adversities, let us bear in mind this truth, that all our thoughts will ever wander and go astray until we are fully persuaded that God alone is sufficient for us, so that he may become alone our heritage. For all who are not satisfied with God alone are immediately seized with impatience whenever famine oppresses them, or sword threatens them, or any other grievous calamity. And for this reason Paul also says, 'If God be for us, who can be against us? . . . I am persuaded that neither famine, nor nakedness, nor sword, nor death, nor life, can separate me from the love of God which is in Christ' (*Rom.* 8:31, 35–39). Then Paul lays hold of the paternal favour of God as a ground of solid confidence . . . Why? Because God is the life [of the faithful] in death, their light in darkness, their rest in war and tumult, their abundance in penury and want . . . none hope in God but those who build on his paternal favour alone, so that they seek nothing else but to have him propitious to them. It afterwards follows:

The LORD is good unto them that wait for him, to the soul that seeketh him (*Lam.* 3:25).

96

We hence see that the last verse is confirmed, where he said that he was content with God alone, while suffering all kinds of adversity: How so? For God, he says, is *good to those who wait for him*. It might have been objected and said that adversities produce sorrow, weariness, sadness, and anguish, so that it cannot be that they retain hope who only look to God alone; and it is no doubt true that, when all confess that they hope in God, they afterwards run here and there; and the consequence is that they fail in their adversities . . . [the Prophet] gives indirectly this answer, that God is good to those who wait for him . . . for God will at length show his kindness to all those who hope in him. In short, the Prophet teaches us here that the blessings of God, by which he exhilarates his own children, cannot be separated from his mercy or his paternal favour . . .

As, then, God deals bountifully with all who hope in him, it follows that they cannot be disappointed, while they are satisfied with him alone, and thus patiently submit to all adversities. In short, the Prophet teaches here what the Scripture often declares, that hope maketh not ashamed (*Rom.* 5:5).

But the second clause must be noticed: for the Prophet defines what it is to hope in God when he says that he is good to *the soul that seeks him* . . . We must then remember what the Prophet says here, that they alone hope in God who from the heart seek him, that is, who acknowledge how greatly they need the mercy of God, who go directly to him whenever any temptation harasses them, and who, when any danger threatens them, flee to his aid, and thus prove that they really hope in God. It now follows:

> It is good that a man should both hope and quietly wait for the salvation of the LORD (*Lam.* 3:26).

. . . the Prophet here reminds us that we are by no means to require that God should always appear to us, and that his paternal favour should always shine forth on our life. This is indeed a condition sought for by all; for the flesh inclines us to this, and hence we shun adversities. We, then, naturally desire God's favour to be manifested to us. How? In reality, so that all things may go on prosperously, that no trouble may touch us, that we may be tormented by no anxiety, that no danger may be suspended over us, that no calamity may threaten us . . . but in such a case faith would be extinguished, as Paul tells us in his Epistle to the Romans, 'For we hope not for what appears, but we hope for what is hidden' (*Rom.* 8:24–25). It is necessary in this world that the faithful should, as to outward things, be miserable, at one time exposed to want, at another subject to various dangers – at one time exposed to reproaches and calumnies, at another harassed by losses: why so? Because there would be no occasion for exercising hope, were our salvation complete. This is the very thing which the Prophet now teaches us, when he declares that it is good for us to learn in silence to wait for the salvation of God.

But to express more clearly his mind, he first says, *He will wait*, or hope. He teaches the need of patience, as also the Apostle does in *Heb.* 10:36; for otherwise there can be no faith. It hence appears that, where there is no patience, there is not even a spark of faith in the heart of man. How so? Because this is our happiness, to wait or to hope; and we hope for what is hidden. But in the second clause he explains himself still more clearly by saying, *and will be silent*. To be silent means often in Scripture to rest, to be still; and here it signifies no other thing than to bear the troubles allotted to us, with a calm and resigned mind. He is then said to be silent to God who remains quiet even when afflictions supply occasions for clamouring; and hence this quietness is opposed to violent feelings; for when some trouble presses on us, we become turbulent, and are carried away by our fury, at one time we quarrel with God, at another we pour forth various complaints . . . and hence the words of Isaiah, 'In hope and silence'; for he there exhorts the faithful to patience, and shows where strength is, even when we trust in God so as willingly to submit to his will, and to be ready to bear his chastisements, and then when we doubt not but that he will be ready to bring us help when we are in danger (*Isa.* 30:15).

We now perceive what the Prophet means when he says that it *is good if we wait and be silent as to the salvation of God;* even because our happiness is hid, and we are also like the dead, as Paul says, and our life is hid in Christ (*Col.* 3:3). As then it is so, we must necessarily be silent as to God's salvation, and cherish hope within, though surrounded with many miseries.